Simply Science

WONDERFUL WATER

Gerry Bailey and Steve Way

Illustrations: Steve Boulter & Q2A Media

Diagrams: Karen Radford

AUTHORS: **GERRY BAILEY**
STEVE WAY
EDITOR: **FELICIA LAW**
ILLUSTRATORS:
STEVE BOULTER
Q2A MEDIA
DESIGN: **RALPH PITCHFORD**

ISBN 978-1-906292-23-2
Printed in China

PHOTO CREDITS:

p.4-5 Elisei Shafer/Shutterstock Inc.
p.8 (t) Ronnie Howard/Shutterstock Inc.,
(b) Dale Mitchell/Shutterstock Inc.
p.9 (cl) Nataliya/Shutterstock Inc.,
(c) Sarah Pettegree/Shutterstock Inc.
p.16 Jubal Harshaw/Shutterstock Inc.
p.17 Can Erdem Satma/Shutterstock Inc.
p.18 Eric Gavaert/Shutterstock Inc.
p.19 Jarvis Gray/Shutterstock Inc.
p.21 Bartosz Wardzinski/Shutterstock Inc.
p.22-23 (t) Vera Bogaerts/Shutterstock Inc.,
(b) Josef F. Stuefer/Shutterstock Inc.
p.24-25 Ulrike Hammerich/Shutterstock Inc.
p.25 (tr) Harris Shiffman/Shutterstock Inc.,
(b) Piotr Sikora/Shutterstock Inc.
p.27 Wade H. Massie/Shutterstock Inc.
p.29 Hulton-Deutsch Collection/CORBIS

Cover
Dale Mitchell/Shutterstock Inc.

WONDERFUL WATER

Contents

What is water?

Water is the clear runny liquid that comes out of the tap when we turn it on. It's the liquid that's in the seas and oceans and in lakes and rivers. It's in the air, when it rains or snows.

When we think of water we think of...
splashing...
puddles...
waves...
swimming...
and diving.

The colourful underwater world that is a coral reef.

Water is all around us. In fact there's more water on the surface of our planet than anything else - about 70%. Oh, and there's more water in us than anything else as well. We're over 60% water!

When lots of things happen over and over again, and in the same way, we call it a cycle. When it ends, it begins all over again – a bit like you going to school every day! Well, water has a cycle as well. And, not surprisingly, it's called the water cycle.

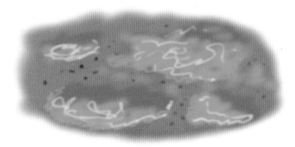

It begins with all the water that's lying around on the Earth's surface, from huge seas and oceans to tiny puddles. When the Sun warms the water, some of it evaporates, or turns into water vapour.

Clouds

Water vapour is very light so it rises up into the air. As it rises it begins to get cooler and eventually changes back into tiny drops of liquid water. This is called condensation. Lots of tiny drops together are called a cloud.

clouds form

Water vapour

Like all things, water is made up of tiny bits called molecules that are always moving about. The hotter something is, the faster the molecules move. If they move quickly enough, some molecules break away from the water and go into the air. These molecules of water are called water vapour, and when they move out of the water, it's called evaporation.

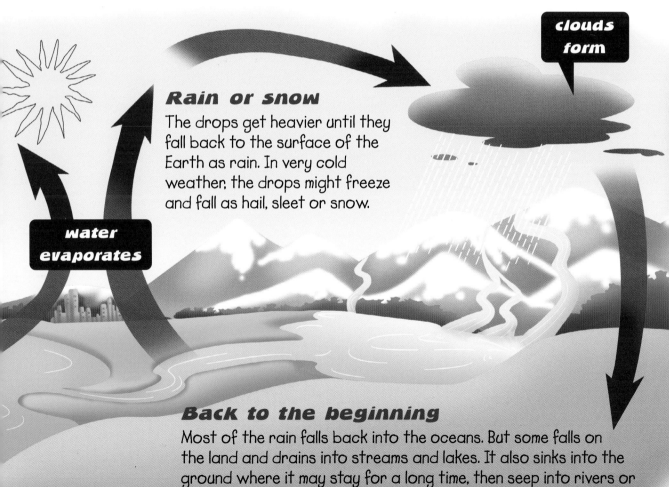

clouds form

Rain or snow

The drops get heavier until they fall back to the surface of the Earth as rain. In very cold weather, the drops might freeze and fall as hail, sleet or snow.

water evaporates

Back to the beginning

Most of the rain falls back into the oceans. But some falls on the land and drains into streams and lakes. It also sinks into the ground where it may stay for a long time, then seep into rivers or come out as a spring. Then the whole water cycle, begins again.

Rivers

People have always relied on rivers to provide water to drink and to act as a transport system for boats and other craft. They're also great to swim in!

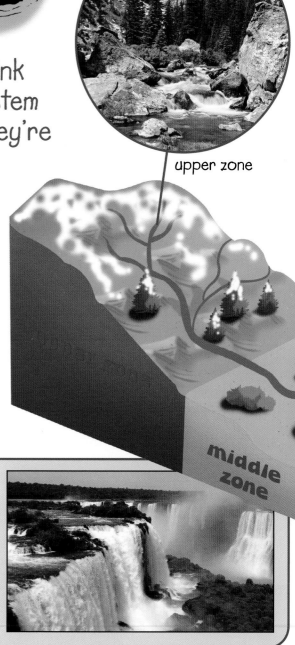

upper zone

middle zone

Springs and streams

Rivers can come from springs that flow from the ground. Or they may begin as tiny streams filled by the rain that's fallen on the hillsides around about. So most rivers begin their life high on the slopes of a mountain or in hilly areas.

Running water

We all know that gravity pulls us down onto the surface of the Earth. But gravity also makes rivers possible. A river is a stream of water that runs downhill, pulled by the force of gravity. The steeper it falls, the faster it runs. Sometimes the water falls over a rocky ledge and becomes a waterfall.

River zones

Scientists divide rivers into three zones. The upper zone is where the river starts. Usually it runs quickly here and can be very cold. It's probably at its cleanest too.

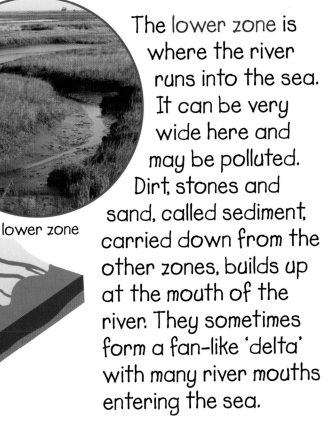

The middle zone is where the river begins to slow down. Lots of wildlife, including fish, birds and animals, live in this zone.

middle zone

The lower zone is where the river runs into the sea. It can be very wide here and may be polluted. Dirt, stones and sand, called sediment, carried down from the other zones, builds up at the mouth of the river. They sometimes form a fan-like 'delta' with many river mouths entering the sea.

lower zone

lower zone

Plants need water

How can I get the river water to the plants in my field?

Long ago, people learned it was possible to plant vegetables and grain to provide food for themselves. Now they didn't have to hunt wild animals all the time and they could settle in one place. But plants need water and sometimes the rainfall wasn't enough.

Water from the river

1. The Ancient Egyptians settled along the Nile River. There wasn't much rain in Egypt so crops needed water brought from the river.

2. But most of the plants the farmers planted were far from the riverbank. They had to think of a way of carrying the precious water some distance from the river to the fields.

Farming

When early people began to farm the land, they were dependent upon finding water close by for their plants. Historians have discovered that farming began along river banks all over the world.

3. First of all they invented a machine called a shadoof. The shadoof worked as a lever to haul water out of the river and up over the riverbank.

4. Then the water was poured into long ditches that ran along the side of and into the fields of crops. Bringing water to crops in this way is called irrigation.

Humans need water

Animals need water just as much as plants do. And because humans are a kind of animal, we need water as well. We wouldn't last very long without it!

We use water to wash in. Ancient people kept themselves clean by washing in rivers and lakes. Luckily we don't have to. We have baths!

People need water to drink. As we're mostly made of water, we have to keep topping it up when we lose it – such as when we sweat or go to the loo.

We also use water for cooking.

Some people get their best ideas in the bath!

The Ancient Romans built huge baths that lots of people could use at the same time. Some baths were heated. You could jump from a very hot bath into a cold one.

Before the invention of antibiotics and other medicines, hot water helped to keep wounds clean.

Breathing in water

Unless you're a fish, you probably find it hard to breathe in water! But when people wanted to explore under the sea, they had to find a way of taking air with them.

Take a deep breath...

1. Some divers can hold their breath underwater for a very long time. But they still have to come up for air at some point.

2. Of course, if you can't actually breathe under water the next best thing would be to take some air with you. You could make an air sac, or perhaps put a helmet full of air over your head...

A diving bell

A diving bell is a large hollow container filled with air and with an air pipe going to the surface. It can be used to carry divers and their tools to work on the ocean floor or to explore the seabed.

3. Better still, you could pump air down to your mouth through a pipe. But how would this work exactly? Edmund Halley had the answer.

4. He built a diving bell that was weighted, so it would sink, and open at the bottom. It could be lowered about 20 metres and divers could stay down, breathing in its oxygen supply, for over an hour.

Water creatures

Millions of years ago all creatures lived in the water. Today many animals still live there, including fish, mammals, amphibians and others.

Fish

Some deep-sea fish have specially designed mouths so they can feed off material they find on the ocean bottom. The viperfish has an extra joint in its head to increase its bite, while the slackjaw has no floor to its mouth.

Mammals

Whales and the dolphins are both mammals. Although they live in the sea, they cannot breathe underwater so they have to come up for air – just like humans do.

These fossils, found buried deep in ancient rocks, show that fish were living on Earth over 50 million years ago.

Amphibians

Frogs are amphibians. They begin their lives as tadpoles that live only in the water. When they change into frogs, they are able to live on land as well as in the water.

Crustaceans

The lobster belongs to a group of animals called crustaceans. They have a hard outer shell on their bodies to protect them from predators.

Reptiles

This snapping turtle is known for its bad temper. And it's a ferocious fighter if it's threatened. It eats fish, plants and even small mammals.

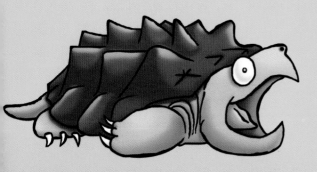

Every part of a lobster's body is protected by hard shell.

Waves

The water in the seas and oceans is moving all the time. On the surface the water moves up and down in waves. When a wave reaches the shore, it moves forward and breaks over the sand.

When the sea gets rough or stormy, the waves push boats up and down, not forwards or backwards.

Ocean waves

Waves are caused by the winds that blow over the surface of the ocean. The faster the wind, the bigger the waves become. It's the wave that moves forward, though, not the water. Underneath a wave, the water is moving in a circle as well as up and down. It only moves forward when it reaches the shore.

Sometimes huge waves, called tsunamis, are created by earthquakes on the seabed. The waves rush at great speed across the water, getting bigger and bigger as they move along. When they reach shore, they break like an ordinary wave, but can cause terrible destruction.

Hot water

When water comes out of a tap, or sloshes about in a pool, it's obviously runny. It's a liquid. But water isn't always a liquid. It can be solid, or it can be a gas. But it's still water.

Water turns to gas when it's heated to 100 degrees Centigrade. At that temperature, it boils. You can see it happen when you boil a kettle. So we say the boiling point of water is exactly 100 degrees C.

Heating water

Water is made up of tiny moving bits called molecules – just like everything else. When the molecules are heated up, they get more active and begin to move faster. The hotter the water gets, the faster the molecules move. They also get further away from each other and start to take up more space. Eventually they're so active that the water is no longer a runny liquid but a cloud-like gas.

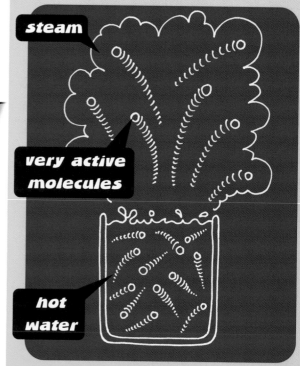

steam

very active molecules

hot water

Geyser

In some places, heat and water from inside the Earth's crust escape through a hole or crack in the surface. They hiss out in a fierce burst of steam called a geyser.

Cold water

Just as water can become a steamy gas when it's hot, it can also change into a solid form when it's cold. We know solid water as ice, frost or snow.

Cooling water

If heating water makes molecules move faster, then cooling it must make them slow down. And it does. In fact, the cooler it gets, the slower the molecules move, until they're hardly moving at all. This time the runny water becomes very hard ice. It's solid now. Water becomes solid, or turns to ice, at 0 degrees Centigrade.

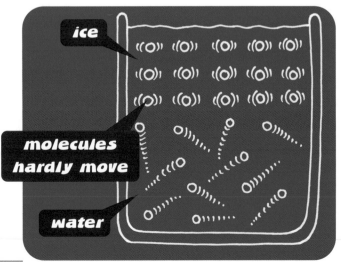

ice

molecules hardly move

water

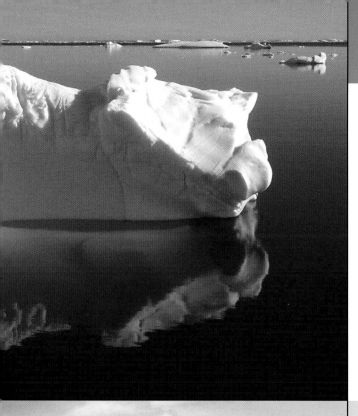

Icebergs

Icebergs are huge lumps of ice. They have broken off the ends of the glaciers or ice sheets that cover the polar regions. When water becomes ice and swells up, it becomes lighter and less dense than liquid water, which is why it floats.

Glaciers

A glacier is a vast river of ice which moves very slowly along a valley. As it moves along it grinds away at the valley reshaping it into a U-shape.

Water supply

Although people need a supply of water to stay alive, they don't always live close to one. People in the desert, for instance, have to hunt for water at oases.

A better way to make sure there's a supply of water is to build some kind of long-distance pipe or trench to run the water along. The Ancient Romans built water-carrying ditches called aqueducts. Aqua was the Roman word for water. Aqueducts crossed deep valleys using an arched bridge.

Later, water was channelled along underground pipes. These not only carried fresh water to people's homes, but a set of different pipes carried the used water away.

This famous Roman aqueduct is the Pont du Gard in France. It was built over 2,000 years ago, to bring water from springs near Uzès to the Roman city of Nîmes. In all, it has 52 great arches.

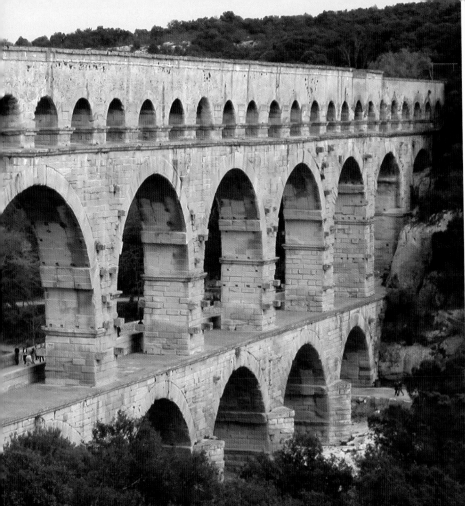

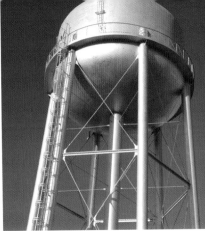

A water tower is a water tank built on high stilts. These towers are constructed so that the supply of water has a long way to drop. The extra pressure this fall creates, helps move the water around a system of pipes.

An oasis is a place in the desert where water trapped far below the ground, rises to the surface. Travellers rely on these springs for water, as do plants and animals. A wadi is a dry river bed that floods only when it rains.

Cleaning water

Water has to be cleaned before it is safe to drink. Some water comes from rivers, lakes and reservoirs. But in parts of the world where water is scarce, it must be re-used and cleaned over and over again.

Dirty water from reservoirs, wells, rivers or lakes is pumped to a water treatment plant. Here, the dirty water passes through a series of tanks which extract the dirt.

How it works

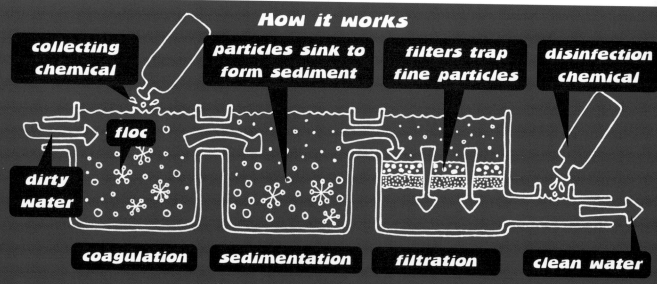

collecting chemical

particles sink to form sediment

filters trap fine particles

disinfection chemical

floc

dirty water

coagulation

sedimentation

filtration

clean water

1. In the first tank a chemical is added which makes small particles of dirt stick together to form scum known as floc.

2. In the second tank the floc and smaller particles settle at the bottom forming a sediment which is regularly cleaned away.

3. In the third tank filters, made from layers of fine coal and sand, trap the remaining dirt particles.

4. Finally a disinfecting chemical is added before the clean water is pumped to a holding tank and from there on to your home.

Dirty water is known as sewage and must be thoroughly cleaned in a sewage plant. This series of tanks moves the water through one process to the next, cleaning it little by little, as it goes along.

2. Some houses had outside toilets called water closets. But they smelled bad too. Something had to be done. John Harington had invented a kind of flush toilet during the reign of Queen Elizabeth I of England. She even had one installed in one of her palaces.

1. Before the flush toilet was invented people used chamber pots. Often chamber pots were emptied out of an upstairs window forcing anyone walking below to duck! This made a terrible mess and wasn't at all sanitary.

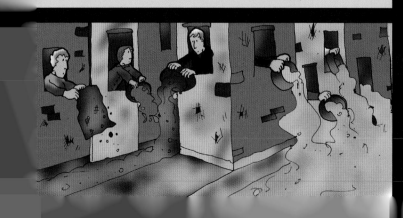

3. Then in the late 1700s Joseph Bramah invented a better toilet. He put a tank of water above the toilet with pipes and openings that connected it to a cess pit.

4. Later, networks of pipes called sewers were built under cities. The water carried sewage from the toilet into the underground network and away from the towns.

Flushing water

Foul waste from our toilets and sewage water from our bathrooms and kitchens, is carried away in separate sewer systems.

Machines help to take out oils, grease, fats, sand and large solid materials such as rags, sticks or cans, from the waste water. This step is done with machinery and is known as mechanical treatment. From now on, the waste will be treated with chemicals.

Sewers are huge pipes and tunnels that usually run under the streets in towns and cities.

Water Quiz

1. What is another name for a material that is runny?

_____

2. What is a cloud made up of?

_____

3. In which direction do waves move?

_____

4. How much of the surface of the Earth is covered in water?

_____

5. What do crustaceans have to protect them from hungry predators?

_____

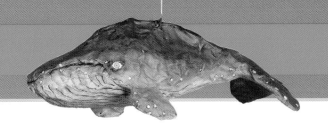

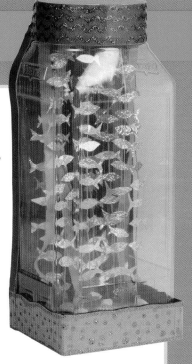

6. What do we call the place where steam spouts from the Earth's crust?

---

7. Why does ice float on water?

---

8. How did the Ancient Romans get water to towns?

---

9. What does a water closet, or toilet, empty into today?

---

10. At what part of a river does a delta form?

1. A liquid 2. Water droplets 3. Up and down and around in a circle 4. Over 70 per cent 5. An outer skeleton 6. A geyser 7. Because it is less dense, or lighter 8. They built aqueducts 9. A sewer 10. At the mouth of a river the lower zone

31

Index